Letters I'll Never Send

By
Cierra Antoinette

© Copyright 2019 by Cierra Antoinette –
All rights reserved.

It is not legal to reproduce, duplicate or transmit any part of this document in either electronic means or printed format. Recording of this publication is strictly prohibited.

Dedications

This book is dedicated to a few different people and times:
To all the people who've crossed my path but are no longer walking the same one. To the imprint that you left on me, the moments we've shared, both good and bad & the memories I'll forever cherish. Love was never lost.

A dedication to all my lowest points & overcoming them. A battle constantly being fought with each breath I take. This is proof that I am greater than it all. I once read that the universe only gives you what you are missing and sometimes what we're missing isn't worth it. This book, this accomplishment makes it all worth it

A dedication and thank you to Kavia, Taylor, Kia, Aliyah, Jabril, Kevon, Jonathan & finally my mother. You all have been a support system like no other, from my lowest points to my peaks. From when I felt like nothing to feeling absolutely amazing. No judgment or transgressions, just pure love. I appreciate each one of you and all you've been through with me. Thank you to my other friends, family, clientele, and people who inspired and pushed me. It's because of you this thought came to fruition.

Also, a dedication to Dezz, Dionne, Q, Duck, and a few others. Some of these were written with you in mind. Thank you for the lessons I didn't know I needed. Thank you for the growth through pain and love. Thank you for understanding me when I didn't even understand it myself. Thank you for giving me inspiration.

A special thank you to whoever is reading this too. I hope I've found a way to speak my truth while helping someone find the words to speak their own. Someone wise once said, "Pain is inevitable, but suffering is optional." Being hurt doesn't mean you have to live in that hurt, life comes with high's and low's, and nothing or no one defines you but you.

If I close my eyes today or tomorrow, my last wish would be to have changed someone else's life for the better. If I know I made at least one person's life better, I will rest eternally at peace. My aspiration is to be an inspiration

- *Cierra Antoinette*

Letters I'll Never Send

You know why I write letters I'll never send?
Sometimes it's because I feel like the recipient won't care.
Sometimes it's because I believe that writing will somehow make it all make sense.
Other time's it's because I feel like maybe I'll find the answer within myself.
Recently though, it's because they don't get a choice.
You see I used to write these letters for answers and validation,
to feel like I was enough to fight for.
Letters because I didn't want to be annoying by sending a paragraph that wasn't going to receive a response anyway
But not anymore.
I don't get to be reeled back in by the same promises as empty as their hearts.
I don't get to be an option to your "I'm not ready, but you are what I want."
I don't get to be made into the antagonist for picking me
Or for choosing to genuinely be happy.
Not this time.
These letters could very well not mean shit to anyone else.
They could be read by the recipients and discarded,
They can bring up questions and trigger conversations.

Hopefully, you find peace in all these things.
These letters are my peace.
These letters are me letting go.
These letters are by me, for me,
They may be to you,
But please understand these are letters I'll never send
Because your response no longer has a bearing on how I chose to heal.

Ode

This poem is a eulogy to who I once was and a dedication to the woman I've become.

One
Ode to the victim. I was pried open at 4 years old. My innocence a trophy for him and I was reminded repeatedly for 4 years. In that time, often I spent time on my knees and God knows I wish it were for prayer. I bathed until my skin peeled, but nothing could wash away the disgust I felt for myself inside. It's been almost two decades... two decades and I'm still afraid of a man getting too close to me.

Two.
Ode to the grade schoolgirl. Academically exceeding in excellence while excelling in extracurricular activities. I had played 9 different sports by the time I was 16. I had picked up 4 different instruments, danced and managed to reach the first chair trumpet. Nobody realized how voided I was, not even myself. Placing my focus into things as a distraction from what was really bothering me.

Three.
Ode to the church girl. I remember the day my OG found out I was a lesbian. My mom wasn't upset at me loving women, just that I didn't tell her. A few Sunday's later I remember going to church with my OG and

them "praying the demons out of me." Acceptance is vital to a child. Unconditional love regardless of personal views is vital to a child.

Four.
Ode to the unrealistic hopeless romantic. I remember my first heartbreak like it was yesterday. I cried for 3 days, refused to eat, and made myself sick. Looking back, I wish everyone would've just let me be. I wish they would've just let me heal on my own instead of saying "I told you so."

Five.
Ode to the naïve. I hate that my mom sheltered me from the world because it made me gullible as hell. I know that she did was she thought was best but baby book smarts amount to nothing in these streets and there are things in life a classroom cannot prepare you for.

Six.
Ode to the statistic. I was 14 when I realized my grandmother had her first child at 13, my aunt had her first child at 15 and my mother had me at 17. You couldn't tell me about this "tradition". I refused to be pregnant at 19. Somehow that would've been more welcomed than me liking women.

Seven.
Ode to the innocent. She's grown into the ethereal. They say heartbreak makes you bitter and pain makes you better. But they never teach you how to harness and harvest it. See we've all had our fair share of pain. I've had fewer highs than someone smoking for the first time and more lows than I care to remember. I have scars engraved in permanent ink on and in me. I have moments where I've had to cleanse within and pray out the pain. But despite it all, I made it. And I'm damn proud.

Remembrance

I remember everything about you
I remember our first conversation along with the promises and plans we made
How the butterflies in my stomach were once caterpillars until you gave them the courage to be beautiful.
You gave me the courage to be beautiful.
I remember how we faded and how I wanted you to save me.
…why couldn't you save me?
Honestly, you still cross my mind.
The way we met and connected instantly.
The way you cared for me.
My smile still carries you.
My pen still writes for you.
My schedule never too busy to fit you and.

I know better…
I know I deserve better,
But I also know you can be better.
Call me crazy but I still have hope.
The truth is I wish you cared more about me.
… I wish I cared less about you.
I wish the memories we had were still only things I dreamt about
Maybe It was wanting you for so long and losing you so quickly.
Maybe it was the questions I ask myself like "what did I do wrong? Why wasn't I enough?"
Even though I was good to you.
Savored you like the last bit of food from a meal I knew I'd never get again
Prayed for you more than myself
Used the last bit of strength in me to try and save you
But I'm no superwoman.
Hell, I even took you to meet my dad.
Some memories I can deal with,
Like the way, your lips felt against mine
Or the way your tongue traced my spine
Or the way you looked at me from behind
Those memories are my pleasure
Our conversations are my pain
How do you get someone to bare their soul to you just to abandon them?
You started reading my book the left me unattended without so much as a warning.
The way they leave always tells you everything

You left me lying in my ruin and although
I've picked myself up, a part of me is still
lying there…
I remember you in a way I shouldn't.
In a way, I wish never existed.
I remember you way more than I wish I did.

Truth

The truth is, I write poems about you
Not the kind I'll ever let you read or
I'll ever say aloud to you because I don't want
to move too fast.
I'm just a writer.
I put my feelings on pen and paper.
I use my words to create a poem.
I can't force a poem…
I can't force something I don't feel…
So, if you ever wonder how I feel about you

Ask to read my poetry.

A Poet's Trilogy
A Poet's Epiphany (Part I.)

I remember the first time I saw you.
I was a shadow in the corner,
A backdrop in comparison to the beauty in the room but nothing…
Nothing compared to you
Maybe it was the mixture of alcohol and my lack of inhibitions
Maybe it was me stepping out of my comfort zone, but I knew I had to take the chance.
I don't know where it progressed but some way, somehow between then and now I've learned 17 different ways to say I love you.
I've learned 9 ways to calm you from your anxiety attacks, I've wipes 289 tears from your eyes, and I've opened my heart up to you like I did no other.
I didn't plan on my heart chakra allowing you to open me up…
But somehow it happened
But what about the other parts of me?
I am not an immaculate girlfriend and I am not an impeccable woman.
I have scars that cut so deep, my soul is still hemorrhaging.
I have walls built from pain and deception.
I have broken bread and butter, bent over backward and given my heart to women who

loved women who have loved people who didn't even care about us.
I stand 4'10 1/2, my stomach is not flat, my muscles are bigger than your average woman's.
I have 9 piercings, 3 tattoos,
an abundance of bruises from my childhood and skin discoloration in the oddest places.
You can't look at me like this is new skin or treat me like this is a new soul.
I have a past that I can't abandon because it made me who I am today.
I have secrets riveted in the deepest valleys of my memory.
I have insecurities that cling to me like a child on monkey bars.
See, I'm not perfect.
Hell, on some days I'm not even good enough.
So, before you take on the task of loving me, can you handle it?
Can you handle the parts of me that welt and bruise?
The parts of me that some may find grotesque and overwhelming.
Can you handle the parts of me that crack like a levy and shatter like glass?
Can you take that journey to the darkest parts of me?
Can you love me then?
What about the parts that are abstruse and bleak?
The parts you can't fathom.

See, you've fallen in love with my flowers but what about my roots?
What about the parts of me I've concealed without acknowledgment?
The scars I've bandaged but never allowed to heal?
When you realize that my flowers wither away in the winter…
When you realize that my mask isn't permanent, and it cracks…
When you realize I'm put together like a game of Jenga,
Every piece you pull is a gamble but my love, remove the right one and I will fall like the London Bridge…
Will you still want me then?

A Poet's Blues (Part II)

It's 3:34 in the morning and you've crept back into my head.
I miss you.
Not the relationship, but I miss you.
Is it possible to be over someone but still drawn to them?
To still have an open spot for them even if you've been hurt.
It's like…
No matter how much damage you did to my flowers, a part of my roots still wants you.
I miss having someone who knew me like the back of their hand.
Who could tell when something was wrong with me without even being there, that connection.
Who already knew what I'd gone through and knew just what to say to make me feel better
And it's like, when I finally feel okay, you pop up doing small shit like liking a tweet or a picture but when I reach out, you retract like you don't want my friendship.
Like we're magnets of the same side repelling and it makes me feel crazy.
Yet, with the same heart you tore apart,
If you were to walk back into my life right now…
I'd put it back in your hands, bandages, and all.

Every single crack and gap in it like a Haitian sidewalk,
I'd give it to you.
Every piece that you abandoned on the ground,
I'd pick up and bare for you to see.
I'd allow the very thing that broke me to make me whole again.
I'd give myself all over again like I was walking down a church aisle to be saved.
I'd let go of all the pain from before like my sins at the altar, in hopes to resurrect as someone whole again.

It's now 4:26 in the morning…
I spent the last hour traveling down memory lane to come to the abrupt dead end that was us
It's crazy how you can travel a road until there's nothing left and still find yourself becoming a construction worker to build more of the path ahead…
I must've counted how many moments I'd take back and change or rewind
Just to give us a little bit more time
Just to be able to call you mine
How many tears I wouldn't have cried,
all the times we spent arguing would've been spent laughing.
Should've and could've wouldn't exist because they'd be replaced with "I did's"

See, I'd go back to a time where your eyes lit up whenever you saw me or when I could hear you smile over the phone
To when everything made sense
To when it was "perfect"
It's 4:34 in the morning and I spent the last hour traveling down memory lane to come to the abrupt end that was us.
And while I was traveling and picking out things that didn't belong,
And the spots where everything went wrong…
As I got to the end of memory lane, I realized that the only place where you and I ever had the perfect ending was in my poetry

A Poet's Healing (Part III)
I craved a change.
19 and lost,
Empty and searching in the wrong places
when I wasn't even sure what I was looking
for.
I spent nights crying and days longing.
See, they tell you that you need love but don't
tell you that you need it from yourself first.
I was young until I was old.
Weak until I was strong.
I gave pieces of myself until I was left whole.
Cried rivers and lakes,
Watched the time pass by until the hands on
my clock had arthritis.
Some days I didn't move out of bed, other
days I distracted myself so much I didn't make
it to bed.
I spent forever searching for myself in women
who left me empty, dripping in beg and
sorrow.
I searched in work, in drugs and drinks
I partied to feel surrounded but never felt more
alone than when I was surrounded by a group
of people whom I only knew over a bottle and
a chant of encouragement to shake what my
mama gave me.
I sat in the mirror and begged for change,
grabbed shears, and began to cut my hair.
Each clip a liberation.

Sobbing as I watched past lovers, anxiety, and discontentment hit my bathroom floor.
See I was too busy trying to be an alchemist.
Recreating myself when I never finished developing, to begin with.
See I needed time to mold.
Time to feel, time to heal.
To appreciate where I came from,
Take note of where I am now and prepare for where I'm going.
I was a seed that grew into a flower fully bloomed.
Petals beautifully blossomed.
A bouquet bursting with brilliance and grace.
I was meek until I assorted authority.
Timid until my boldness spoke without my mouth moving.
Insecure in who I was until I realized all I needed was myself.
I look back and I'm able to say that she was good.
But this version of me…
Is damn great.

Desensitization

"I expected it." She said.
"It's okay." She said.
Subtly brushing off the feeling that she had felt time and time again because she was so used to it.
See there was this expectation of love being chaotic no matter who it was from.
No matter the time or essence, or how often she reflected on the presence or the message they left,
It just never led to anything else.
She grew tired of emptying herself out to be disappointed because after doing the same social experiment person after person, she concluded that everyone was the same.
Starting with family and friends,
Drifting into lovers who promised forever with lips that told lies like days of the week.
She grew tired of being weak
So, when it happened, she felt nothing.
As another one walked away,
She prepared for the next few because she knew no one would stay.
And no matter how much she would pray there was always a small voice that reminded her that they're all the same.
It was always the same.
She always felt the same.

My Kind of Love

I'm the kind of love that comes with a warning label
That fucked up kind of love that'll fuck you up too, but in a good way
I'm that "first cup of black coffee" kind of love, strong.
The kind of strength you can't ignore.
I'm that "first hit of a blunt" kind of love.
The newness will hit you in your chest but once you get used to me, you'll always want me around.
I'm not the "hold my hand and tell me I'm pretty" kind of love.
There's nothing wrong with it, it's just not me.
I'm that love like a marbled canvas, messy but beautiful.
I'm that scared kind of love.
Not scared of being hurt, been there done that.
But scared of hurting someone else because I've been there
Excuse me, because I'm still growing and although I know it,
I'm willing to take that chance
I'm that kind of love that doesn't usually get a second chance.
I'll engrave my name on your heart like the 10 commandments in stone,
I'll leave my imprint to remind you that I've been there

I'm the kind of love that is here to show you that we exist,
But I'm only here to exist.
I'm the kind of love that teaches you a lesson.
That's here to help you grow but understand that when you surpass me, love I won't be afraid to let you go.
I'm the love that can be bitter, and darling you deserve better.
So, whatever you do, don't fall for me.
Because I'll catch you, lay you gently on the ground and fade away...
Because my love is here to teach.

Nostalgia

I spend my nights lying awake in the beautiful ruins
Of memories and past lovers.
Nostalgic at the good times we once shared.
I swear … I feel each emotion as if it were that day again

Take My Hand

Take my hand.
I am a reflection of you.
A mirror to the essence of your being
I am a glass half full to your glass half empty
Take my hand and be my guide
Guide me to your brightest moments, your
darkest secrets, and your deepest fears
Give me your hand and let me guide you to
mine
I'm not afraid of much
And I rarely become this invested
But you caught me in a way that makes me
feel like this can't be wrong
Ne Me Quitte Pas, mon ami
You've become my favorite unfinished novel
My "I's" have turned into "we's"
What was mine has turned into ours
Let me be the water fall that continuously
pours into your stream
Let you be the river that keeps me running.
For the sake of us, take my hand

Colors

I dream of you in colors that don't really exist
Pardon me for being a visionary,
But the color wheel doesn't have the shades or hues
To describe the way, I see you
Warm undertones and cool blues clashing beautifully
Beautiful reds over earth browns
It makes no sense, but it doesn't have to
I dream of you in colors that don't really exist
And I don't want to wake up to a realistic color wheel.

Stagnant

She said she cared.
I remember hearing the same promises escape
from different women like a scratched record
on my phonograph.
A realistic perception of meeting the same
people in different bodies.
I'm starting to believe that my gullibility is
worn on my sleeve, much like my emotions
And I should know better by now.
Maybe it's my need to see the good in people,
Even when I know the shit isn't there.
I just don't understand how the same person
who makes me feel invincible…
Can treat me like I'm invisible.
Now I could play the blame game, but the
fault is just as much mine as anyone else's.
Them constantly spilling what they knew
would get to me was only because I listened.
Only because I was taught to say what I mean,
so I swore others did the same.
And that doesn't make either of us right or
wrong,
It just makes us incompatible.
It makes you another amount of invested time
that I wasted,
Another number added to the same lesson
being retaught because I failed to learn the last
time.
And it makes me stagnant.

Last Night

Last night I dreamt that somebody loved me.
They held the frail thing that was my heart in their hands and reminded me that there is beauty in life after all
Kissed my forehead, nose and chin, the holy trinity
Comforted the very essence of my being
Lied silently beside me as our hearts created the perfect love song
They stayed for the parts of me that even I hated.
Gave support, patience, and understanding.
Allowed me to be myself because I am whole without them
We don't need one another to "complete" one another.
We just complement one another so well that it makes sense.
Everything made sense.
Last night I dreamt that somebody loved me.
And lately, my dreams have been coming to fruition

Prelude

In my 21 years of living, I've written more than I can count.
Memo's, poems, notes to myself and others,
Notebooks filled with prayers
And one love letter.
I'm a hopeless romantic
Don't believe I'm the prettiest,
But I do believe my love is everlasting.
Wise beyond looks,
A nurturing soul regardless
So why only one love letter?
For me, feelings become more real once I express them.
They become aggressive.
They become tattooed on my arm for the world to see
It's like bringing them to fruition.
So once again, why only one love letter?
Because it was that letter that opened the doors to my first heartbreak.
But it also turned me into the woman I am today. It's what leads to a lot of this poetry.
And I'm honestly sick of writing about heartbreak.

Penitent

I am not a victim.
I think we often tell one-sided stories
Or we make excuses for ourselves and our wrongdoings.
You see, I've also been every one of the people I've written about
I've put someone through these emotions
And whether intentional or not, I did it.
I've broken women like pencil lead
Promised to be strong and sturdy then snapped apart without warning
Used their emotions as a lottery ticket and gambled my love
Waiting for better just in case it came along.
See I always stayed on my feet for "the one" but I never fully invested because I was unsure.
The first time I had my heart broken was by a woman I'd hurt twice beforehand
Call me crazy, but I was upset.
The audacity of you to hurt me when I was finally ready to commit
Never mind the fact that I'd been teetering all this time just in case.
I had some nerve
Took me some months to stop pitying myself, stand up and give me a reality check.
Sometimes I look back to see who I was back then
And truthfully, I don't know.

But she needed that heartbreak.

See Me

See Me
See me for who I really am
Not the clothing I wear or the style of my hair
The curves of my body, or how "different" I look.
See me.
A lot of people decide that they want me,
But they don't want the experience.
They want the high's and not the lows.
It's frustrating how they come up with this perception,
Of who I am based on how I look.
Or dress
Or what I choose to listen to musically.
I believe everything has layers and phases.
You can't successfully box me into one thing
You can't limit me to just this one group.
Accept and see all of me or just let me be

Fallen

Do you know what it's like to have your soul snatched without a touch?
To have someone look at you with such intensity that the world around you stops?
For each touch, each kiss to send a current of electricity through your body as strong as lightning from the sky?
Words that leave you speechless because you'd discovered a new language.
A vibe that wakes up the "butterflies" that you never knew existed,
Just only heard about and imagined
Do you know what it's like to look at someone and be smitten?
For your breath to get hitched in your chest as you take in every feature.
To understand the beauty.
To know that time was taken to perfect the art that you can see
And only time can be taken to genuinely appreciate all that it is
Do you know what it's like to imagine?
To see a future with someone and it is lucid?
To want the imperfections and minuscule things
That comes with it but to also want to build.
To believe that there must've been some wonderful figure in this world who took the time to make it possible for someone this amazing to cross paths with you.

And it may be temporary, but you will make the best of each second that happens

Do you know what it's like to fall?

Love Jones

I got a little love jones for her
It's not anything too strong but something that makes me want to do no wrong to her
Something that makes me want to vibe along to her…
See she's her own song.
Take lips as soft as Amel Larreiux's voice…
Combine them with hands like a Teddy Pendergrass song, stern, and firm…
But still able to move you.
Give her a heart that samples the acoustic line in '911' by Wyclef
Emotions like Stevie in 'Ribbon in The Sky'
And eyes deeper than the ocean.
It's the smallest things about her.
The way she smiles makes every dormant butterfly in my stomach takes flight
The way she speaks makes me want to hear her read poetry all night long.
The way she blushes reminds me she's still a woman,
She's still soft and in an instant, I want to protect her
I want to explore her mind.
Let her thoughts be a playground and I be an 8-year-old again, I want to know it all.
I want to earn her trust.
I want to earn her opening to me.
I want to become a safe place for her feelings.
Where she comes when it gets rough.

Cierra Antoinette   Letters I'll Never Send

I want to motivate and support her.
Paint a picture using her as a muse and baby,
Picasso couldn't see the beauty.

June 24th

The night she kissed me created a new
dimension for me.
It was warm and muggy outside after an
evening of summer rain.
We had made plans that day, but something
came up, so I was slightly disappointed.
But of course, she pulled through later
We sat in the car and talked about your
dreams.
I watched the streetlight cast a reflection
across your face.
You told me to step out because you wanted to
hug me.
Being in your arms made me feel safe and
secure.
It didn't matter that it was hot as hell and you
had on a hoody and sweats.
It didn't matter that I looked a mess
I felt safe and happy.
I stand 4'10, she 5'8/5'9
So, she lured over me a bit.
Hands pressed around my waist, touch gentle
enough to be a cloud but firm enough that I
knew that she meant it
She looked down at me and smiled
That smile that made my heart skip a beat
I wanted her lips to touch mine, id waited for
so long
I must've gotten sick of waiting and being
nervous because before I knew it,

Cierra Antoinette   Letters I'll Never Send

I pulled her by her hoodie and bought her lips to mine
That night… that night I felt something
Call it cliché but fireworks went off and I felt my heart jump out of my chest.
I felt myself melt into her hands
And at that moment…
I knew I wanted her

1

You were that shooting star in a pitch-black sky,
A refreshing breath of air in tainted lungs.
I fell in love with you the way we fall asleep,
Slowly then all at once
I fell in love with you because you loved me when I couldn't love myself.

Untitled

You had me wrapped around you from your words,
But then I started noticing your actions didn't match up.
And neither did your feelings.
I was just your entertainment.
A placeholder until something spectacular came along
I loved your flowers and in return offered you my roots
But you didn't even wait on the seasons to change
You planted me in the ground and instead gifted me a drought
Your name signed at the bottom.
An ode to what I imagined we would be,
And a promise of every reality I hoped we were not.
Yet, somehow, I found myself pushing with everything in me to open for you each dawn and close for you every dusk…
Why do we make homes out of people we don't plan to keep?
Why do we offer good head, I mean knowledge to people who don't even bother to feign sapiens?
A constant battle of confusion between my heart,
Baby finding errors in Einstein's theory was easier than loving you.

I guess that's why they say love is a science…
And I was too busy trying to be a gardener.

Conversations with self: Excerpts of nightly thoughts

Whenever I feel an overwhelming amount of negative emotion, especially sadness, the first thing I do is go to sleep. I make myself tired or tell myself I'm tired until I fall asleep. I wake up, may check my phone, then repeat this process. This is the beginning of my self-isolation. Truthfully, I didn't even know I isolated myself when I have issues until my best friend pointed it out. I like my isolated time though. It gives me time to think, reflect, remove, and recharge. I can ponder what it is that is bothering me to the point where I need to be alone, or what it is that I need to feel that I'm blocking out. Once I get to that point, I can also reflect on how I even got in that situation or mood. What I could've done differently and not only what was done to me but what part I played. I think a lot of times people try to place blame on others in certain situations, but I believe there's rarely a situation where one person is solely the victim. There are things done on all party's parts and not only that, there are different perceptions. What's done to me, I may perceive one way while someone else may have a completely different recollection of these events. Not the order of events, but in emotions. High emotions cloud judgment so when I reflect, I'm able to look back and see "okay you were feeling this way, so you weren't really hearing them or understanding them." After that, I remove that situation from myself. By that I mean, I acknowledge what I feel and do what needs to be done. If I'm hurting, I feel it and I do what needs to be done to heal. If I'm sad or upset, I feel it and I let it go. Harboring those things only make them fester into something more. I'm tiny, I don't have the space to let things fester. That's tiring and draining in multiple aspects. It's too much. And finally, I recharge. Not just from this process, but overall. Sometimes we give so much of ourselves to people with being social, working, so on and so forth. We need a moment to just give to ourselves. To do what we want without no interruptions, away from the outside world for a bit. Whether that's painting or soaking in a bath with candles and your crystals. Or maybe it's just chilling and listening to music.

Fears

I'm scared…
Right now, I want to be so mad at you.
I am so mad at you.
I want to leave; I want to stay…
I want to simultaneously throw things at you
But I also don't feel like I have the time to be mad at you.
28 days, maybe less than that is what we have left… and I'm scared.
I'm scared that you'll go, and we won't speak.
That I'll detach, and you'll find better.
It may be unorthodox, but I've been there before.
I've been the girlfriend that waits through basic training, never received a letter, got one phone call and in the same breath of excitement to hear her voice, I had nothing to talk about.
A month and a half, and I had nothing to talk about.
I didn't realize I had detached until she was back. and it didn't really matter to me anymore.
I didn't realize when we went all day without talking.
I didn't worry when I didn't get my nightly calls.
I didn't want to share the good news with her first.

So, when I ask for the letters, the calls, the pictures, the reassurance…
It's not because I'm being clingy.
It's because you're everything I've prayed for.
It's because you're a great part of my support system.
It's because you've become my best friend.
It's because you are someone I'm scared to lose.

October 16th

I often wanted to feel something.
Anything.
Because it was better than nothing.
Because numbness equates to being apathetic
& emotions let me know I still have the ability to be empathetic.
But sometimes I feel too much ...
Sometimes I wish I felt nothing.
that I didn't care & that nothing mattered.
That you didn't matter...
I spent nights making mental notes to myself.
"I deserve happiness.
I deserve everything I give.
I'm not obligated to wait on anyone.
I shouldn't ever feel wrong for choosing me."
Because in all actuality,
if you wanted me there would've been consistency,
not just spoken words with no intentions.
And I may still be a little mad,
because of the shit I chose to put up with for the sake of not wanting to lose you.
But I'm more disappointed in me.
because I knew better than what I chose to deal with.
I knew that our "us" had a minimal chance of becoming a "we"
and I knew that there was always a lineup of women
But hell, who was I to turn down what I'd wanted for so long,

especially if you chose me.
Just maybe if I stayed around long enough,

Maybe you'd make me your star player…
Maybe I'd become your MVP.

October 16th Part 2

I rewrote this poem about 4 or 5 times.
It took me a while to formulate sentences that weren't 97% curse words.
It amazes me how you can pour so much into someone and in the light of day realize all they're doing is draining you.
Take a list of things we did wrong and lay them in front of you to follow as your crimes.
Us both judge, jury, and executioner.
Truthfully, I hurt myself expecting you to be as loyal as me.
Let's be honest, consistency was never an attribute you possessed and
Selflessness never outweighed your need to look out for yourself
Egotism was the wave you often chose to ride
And it's almost impossible to care for someone who only cares about themselves.
You can't constantly try to make something meant for you.
I can't constantly keep giving you chance after chance to prove yourself to me.
Romantically and platonically.
I can't expect you to be present for me when you aren't even present for yourself.
I can't expect for my feelings to be taken care of when you pretend your own feelings don't exist.
Patientia comes est sapientiae.
Patience is the company of wisdom.

And it'd be wise of me to realize that maybe we were never friends.
Friends don't abandon friends.
They don't leave them high and dry for a situation they had a hand in.
Maybe we were just two people who enjoyed the same activities that took things further than they were meant to go.
Maybe that was our mistake.
And this isn't a blame game.
It's just ventilation because I can't keep allowing myself to wonder why.
Why you ghosted me this time?
Why you don't reach out?
Why you even pretended to care in the first place?
What was really the point here?
Some questions are better unanswered,
And some don't have answers.
But one thing is for sure…
There was never a logical outcome for us on any level.

Progression

I was fine.
I was fine before you doubled back & stepped foot into my life again.
I was hurt but damnit I had healed, and I was becoming whole again.
Then you came back & reopened this hole again.
How can you do all that work just to go back to square one?
To let all the pain, renew after you've become anew & God, I wish I knew to block you before you came back.
Truthfully, I don't know who I'm more mad at, you or myself.
You knew I'd forgive you... You knew I always had a special place for you
And that a part of me would still wait for you with hopes that you'd grown to become who I knew you had the potential to be.
Hopes that your past scarring would allow you to still hold the possibility of you & me becoming a "we."
Now I'm back in this revolving door of wanting you to want me and working to make you want me when damnit I know you don't deserve me but ...
I always want the things that hurt me.
Even when I know they aren't worthy
Even when I know it's not worth me

.

Conversations with self: Trust

Trust is a very… touchy subject. I feel like a lot of times people try to talk about trust and underestimate just how difficult trusting really is. Especially trying to trust again. Trying to rebuild the trust that's been broken and get to the place where you once were. It's hard. It's stressful. You still go through the ups and downs of what happened. You still live through it. The little piece of you that's always scared. And what's crazy is, you don't understand how hard it is until the trust is broken. You had to let them in when you were already a bit scared. So how do you take steps to trust again? That's a question I didn't have an answer to. I remember once being asked "Do you think trust can be reestablished the way that it was in the beginning?" and for a while, my answer was "yes. If you work hard enough." But I also didn't realize the magnitude of that question. When I was 5, I skinned my knee and elbow on the playground running. I wasn't paying attention and I lost my balance and fell. I'm 21 now, and I still have those scars. I don't think about them all the time. I'm not afraid of running. But I also know "Hey I can hurt myself if I don't pay attention or keep my balance." That's kind of how trust is. You can trust again, but there's always that underlying notion of "pay attention to this, be sure that it doesn't happen again, and you don't get hurt again." And that notion dulls down but it doesn't ever really go away. It doesn't ever really disappear. Especially when you're put back in a situation similar to or just like the one that caused the trust to break in the first place. It's like a voice that's telling you to be scared. To be afraid and worry and wonder what's going on or if this is it all over again. For me, a battle those voices and try to calm myself with things like "this isn't that again. Everything is fine. You're okay. You're loved." You know? Affirmations and positive words. Sometimes I even try to distract myself because I need it. I need to occupy my idle mind because if I don't, these voices and emotions will drown me and drag me back to a place that's a dark time for me. We all have moments we relive and things we never want to feel again. I don't think anyone wants to be back in a position of feeling like "damn I love this person, but I cannot trust them." And that also raises other questions. Like "If you can't trust them, can you truly love them? Can you truly give all of yourself to this person?" That's still something I think about on occasion. I believe it's easy to love someone that you actually trust. I believe it's possible to love someone although you don't trust them. But because of the trust that's missing, how do you progress and where does it lead?

Conversations with self: Healing

I like to fix things that are broken…
Objects, relationships, hearts, people, you name it. I find solace in knowing I helped someone heal and be well again. This doesn't always end well for me. The truth is, I don't have any boundaries when it comes to giving. I'll give my last if it means someone that I care about will be okay. And in the end, I'm left drained. Not saying I do these things for the reciprocity, because it's never that. I just have realized that my "need" to be a good person to others almost always outweighs my need to be good to myself. I like seeing the good in people. I think that every person is or once was a good person, they just became a bit damaged. So, with a little bit of the right things, they'll heal. Almost like a flower, if you water it, give it light, love it then it'll come back to life. Not saying I can heal anyone, but maybe I can push them and hand them a tool belt loaded with the tools to want to heal themselves. Maybe show them that just because they're damaged, they aren't bad. I've realized I'm a natural nurturer and sometimes it attracts people to that'll drain me. But I can't continuously give and give when my cup is empty. I can't give what I don't have. I've learned over the years that I have a problem

with putting myself first because then where do I put the others? Where do I put the people I care about and love? Why do I feel selfish for loving myself enough to say "No" with conviction? Why do I feel guilty for isolating myself to recharge? I'm just getting to a point where I can cancel plans and say no without feeling like I'm being mean or hurting someone's feelings. I feel like I give to everyone but me and it's time for me to heal myself.

Dear You

Dear You,
You are beautiful. I've listened to you sit and pick apart the pieces of you that you don't like, time and time again. I've watched you push away people who possibly loved you because you were afraid. I watched you change. I watched us change. Your pain doesn't make you unlovable. The people who attempted to break you don't make you any less of who you are. The bruises, tangible and emotional, are not your story. Your past trauma doesn't define you. You are enough. You're more than enough for the person meant for you. That's on all levels. You're not broken or damaged. You aren't unlovable. You aren't a burden. You carry magic in yourself. You harness a gift that you don't even realize. What's for you is already yours, you just haven't gotten there yet. You aren't broke or poor, you just haven't reached your rich stage yet. Dear You, thank you for being you. For pouring so much into others without a second thought. For loving hard. For still fighting for the ability to love that hard, despite how many times you get hurt. Keep that pure heart because it is what makes you yourself. You're surrounded by love because you give so much love. You're surrounded by beautiful people who want to see you win and that's something that can't be bought.

Dear You,
Whenever you need a reminder, a pick me up,
a little note to self or you just need to love
yourself more

read this

.

Holy Conversations

I talk to God about you.
I set an appointment with him just to talk about the things you do.
Thank him over and over for putting you into my life.
Kiss Jesus' feet, sacrifice the lamb at the altar, watch the bush burn.
Take a moment to gaze at the beauty he's created in his image.
I talk to God about you.
The conversations may not always be good, but they are always fulfilling.
He lets me know day by day that you were meant to be a part of my life, a part of this life.
That we may have been souls intertwined in another lifetime and found each other in this one as well.
Reminds me that faith without hard work is dead and I have faith in us.
Even if we aren't meant to be romantically, you are my best friend.
I talk to God about you.
I take the moments we have,
both good and bad and write them down in my heart,
engraving them in our story because it hasn't ended yet.
This story ends one of two ways,
Me crossing that threshold and meeting my God on the other side,

Or us not making it that far and being a lesson
in one another's life.
Either way,
I'll still talk to God about you.

Home

Hands intertwined…
I lay my head on your shoulder and admire all that you are.
Take a moment to indulge in the intimacy that is not sexual.
Turn my head to gaze at your face.
The way your eyelashes curl around those almond eyes.
The smooth chocolate layer known as your skin.
The highway that angles your face known as your jawline.
You are breathtaking…
Inhale, exhale
I take time to breathe until my body is no longer tense.
The nervousness fades, but the butterflies in my stomach remain.
The music of your laughter chimes as we joke about 'First 48'
My leg wraps around yours.
My arms find their way around you as I bask in the place called home.
I never understood the saying "home isn't a place but a person." Until this moment.
Home is where you're comfortable, easy, carefree, and safe.
A kiss placed on my forehead
Another on my cheek,

Cierra Antoinette   Letters I'll Never Send

Continuously around my face, as I giggle like a toddler.
Arms wrapped around me that give me no second guess about whether I am protected.
Your scent is intoxicating.
Your lips so sweet it is sinful
We both sit startled that our heartbeats are in sync
Soft kisses on hands while I sit in the passenger's seat
Stop lights and brake lights reflecting on your skin
This is what TLC meant by 'Red Light Special'
I stare at you in awe
You are beauty in human form
An affirmation that everything will be okay
Your jawline clenches as you tense out of habit
My acrylics graze it slowly just to ease you
Wanting to be all for you that you are for me
I know this moment isn't forever…
We'll have to part ways once the sun sets then rises again.
So, I'll enjoy now.
Thank the Highest God that we have these hours between us,
And cherish them as if they'll never happen again.
This feeling anew but I can see why people get so addicted…
I have found my home

To My Future Lover

My name is Cierra. I sometimes go by Ci.
I am a walking contradiction.
I like animals of all sorts and romance novels that make me cry.
I love reading books, especially if it's to other people or if it's raining.
I drink tea before bed and listen to old Billie Holiday records in my room while I paint.
I'm like 65 in a 21-year old's body.
I hate clowns with a passion. I don't like spiders or bugs. I don't sleep as much as I should. My brain is constantly running and sometimes it beats me in the race. I'm a very affectionate being, tangibly and intangibly. I crave being in your presence even if you're doing nothing. I will always want to be touching you in some way. I'll run my fingers along the line of your jaws randomly. Sometimes I'll just stare at you, not to be weird but to take a mental photograph of you and engrave it in my heart. I can be very irrational and moody. When I'm upset, I can't see beyond my emotions. It drives me crazy, but I have a need to feel all my emotions before I use logic. Sometimes that doesn't allow me to see things from your perspective. I don't like to argue. I won't curse at you or raise my voice. I will walk away until I can come back and talk things out logically. I sometimes shut down when I feel too much.

Don't be alarmed, I just need a moment to come to terms with it all.
I'm very short. By very, I mean 4'10 ½. But I am also very self-sufficient. I don't need you to get the flour from the top shelf, I'd rather you watch me struggle and do it on my own. I will be your biggest non-familial fan. I will cheer you on in all your endeavors, if they don't land us in jail, lol.
I don't really believe in the government of marriage but that may change. But I do believe in the union of marriage, so commitment doesn't scare me. Honestly, it does the opposite. It excites me. I want to live in a loft or apartment. Eventually a house, so we have a big family. I want to experience water births surrounded by healing crystals with jasmine flowers in the water. I want to make home videos of our children and have family game nights and bonding nights. I want to eat dinner as a family and hold random talks just to make sure we're all okay.
I get wrapped up in my art at times. I can paint or write all day without remembering to eat or any concept of time. I will use you as a muse. To my future lover, you will become my best friend. I will spend forever wanting to see you smile. I will love you with everything in me. I'll cherish all that you are and all that we build, the good and bad times between us. I will pray for you and with you. I will grow with you and give you space so we can grow

on our own as well. I am walking beside you on a path and while we're unsure whether it's temporary or for the rest of this lifetime, I will care for you from that point beyond.

What does your love taste like?

What does your love taste like?
It is as fulfilling as your lips against mine?
As tender as your touch or as firm of your grasp?
Does it rearrange my guts like you do when you…
tell me you love me.
See I must create room because I've heard you say it a million times,
but I find more butterflies each time you do.
Is it as comforting as you wrapping your arms around me?
Does it smell as good as your cologne, baby let me know...
What does your love taste like?
Is it as homely as the first meal you cooked me?
I don't doubt I'll savor each bite just the same.
Drink from your cup like communion
Pull your hands to mine in prayer,
A Devine entree it is.
What does your love taste like?
Does it quench the thirst most of us have but can't explain?
Does it touch me from miles away and leave me breathless?
Does your love leave me craving when it's gone?

What does your love taste like?

Ellipses

I once asked why 'love' is deemed as such a feminine trait. I was told because it shows weakness. But why is love equated to weakness? I got asked why sex is equated with openness. If I had the answer, I'd tell you. My question still unanswered, a young lady responded, "because it makes you vulnerable." Love is tied to vulnerability, not weakness. Do you know how much strength it takes to be open and bare your soul?

To pour yourself out from within and let every piece of you be viewed as if it's judgment day. You see, love is deemed as a feminine trait because women are strength. Love is strength, Jasmine Mans once said, "Love is the passion that allows you to do the right thing."

Love is what we outpour when there is nothing left to give.

Love isn't a long paragraph; love isn't the nights spent on the phone asleep.

Love is seeing each imperfection and accepting it openly.

Love is realizing just how fucked up someone is and seeing through it.

Love is carrying a child for 9 months, feeling it grow and change daily, going through hours of labor, birthing, nurturing, caring for and raising a child.

See there's no love like a mother's love.

Love is a sacrifice.

Love is what we women were made for.

Cierra Antoinette   Letters I'll Never Send

Let's not forget we were born from the rib of man,
Created as a companion, made to love.
We are NEEDED.
Women are love

.

11:11

I am beautiful.
I am worthy of a love that is healthy and honest.
A peaceful love, a romantic love.
A love filled with trust and compassion.
A partner who understands that we are individuals who complement one another.
Supportive love.
I am love.
All the things I seek, I can give.
I can refill peoples cup as they pour into me.
My loved ones are always protected
We are where we need to be,
Learning what we need to learn to get where we're meant to be.
Things are working in our favor, not against us.
We receive all the blessings that are coming our way.

Ase

Blessed

12:27 am
You lie sleeping a state away
Your soft breathing a lullaby over the phone.
Coupled with memories of the time we just spent together,
I hear the track of my future

Laodicean

More feelings and truth have slipped through your drunken lips than I've ever known from your sober words. Cloaked by wine or tequila, dripping with emotions, and filled with honesty all to be swept under a rug of apathy the next morning. I fell in love with the person under that rug... I know you're somewhere in there…
I just wish you were as ready to face them as I am to love them.

Conversations with self: Life Lessons 2018

2018 was one of my lesser years. But also, one of many lessons. I lost my first apartment. Lost a few friends of many years. I fell to one of my lowest points. But I also gained a lot. I outgrew the energy for unnecessary drama and pettiness because we're grown. Why even entertain that? I also learned about self-worth and making yourself inaccessible to people. It's important to value yourself over 'Love'. By that I mean, when we love someone, we tend to give them certain leverage. We accept things we wouldn't normally accept; we are more lenient with them. And that sometimes puts us in uncomfortable situations. I'm not saying don't be selfless with the people you genuinely love. I'm saying be selfish with you. You can't give pieces of yourself to people who won't even give it back. You can't give someone the shirt off your back who wouldn't even give you a sleeve off that same shirt if you needed it. Second chances are okay to give. What's not okay is allowing a repeat of the same thing to come into play. What's not okay is caring about someone so much you let them take advantage of you. Because that's what happens sometimes. We care about people and we love them so much that we lay out this red carpet and lay on the carpet for them to walk all over us. We don't realize it sometimes, but it happens. Even when we do realize it, we don't want to believe someone we love and care about would ever take advantage of us. Why? Because we wouldn't do that to them. Another life lesson I learned is removal and rekindling. Sometimes people are removed from our lives because our path to travel has come to an end. We can't force relationships of any kind, whether platonic, intimate, etc. Sometimes we find people from our past because they're meant to be in the 'now'. We may even form bonds with people we never thought we'd be that close with. They become people who are important to us. Their well-being, their mental health, how their day was… They become a part of your everyday life and while they don't replace those people, they teach you lessons you had forgotten about yourself. These people are amazing. Even now as I sit typing this, I'm surrounded by smiles, happiness, and love. Unconditional, nonjudgmental, motivational, genuine love. People who encourage me to be the best version of myself I can be in this present moment. They push me in all aspects and genuinely try to understand why I am who I am. Moments like this are priceless.

I learned what I did and didn't want in my life and it started to show. I started to see things a little differently and just realize I wasn't worried about a lot of things other people worry about. I believe everything happens in due time. I believe that there's no such thing as a coincidence and that each person placed in our lives teaches us something. And sometimes, we learn what we are and are not willing to deal with through others. I don't want fame. I don't want 'clout' or 'popularity'. Do I want to be rich? Eh. I'd be more so happy with financial stability and prosperity. I want my soul fed. I want internal knowledge. A small artist loft filled with plants and a meditation room. Occupied by me and the person I love. A cat or a small puppy. A bigger space when our family grows, but nothing wildly big. I also want to live someplace quiet. No place too busy. A porch swing, a front and back yard, a garden. I don't really see the point in a giant house with 9 bedrooms and 5 bathrooms and all of that. To me, it just seems… lonely. And loneliness is not a feeling I'm fond of.

I also learned that when something is removed from your life, don't reopen the door just because you miss them. Don't leave the door ajar for them so they can creep their way back in. Close and lock it on their way out. Because some people only come back because you'll always be there. This is to 2019. This is to doing better for myself, being better for myself and giving myself the things that I deserve

January

This month has been… interesting to say in the least. I've gone through so many emotions and twists and turns, that I feel a bit... out of sorts. My relationship is at stake. Truthfully, I don't know what I'm doing in that damn relationship…

What I've learned though, is that I come first. I spend so much time putting others before myself and when I decide to put me first, I feel guilty. Last night I made a vision board for myself. I set up the things I wanted to achieve. While I want my lover to be a part of it, I also learned that I can't force anything. IF we are meant to be then we will be. If this was a lesson to learn, then that's okay too. But in this lesson, I found my best friend. I learned that I can be loved for who I am. I don't have to sacrifice pieces of myself or dim my light down for anyone to accept me, and if I do, they aren't the person for me. I learned about unconditional love so strong it scares you. I learned about sea legs and nonsexual intimacy that's better than any orgasm. Vulnerability stemming from the connection you have. I felt things that I want to feel for the rest of my life. I learned a beautiful lesson from a beautiful teacher, who also showed me that everything I've been praying for exists. And maybe it's not a lesson, but an experience I get to have for the rest of my life. But whatever it is, I'm grateful I had it. I'm grateful the universe had our paths collide so we could stroll along for the rest of this journey. It may not be hand in hand, and I may not be beside you each step of the way, but you've found a best friend and someone to always cheer you on from the sideline

1:29 am

Speckled glass taints the floors
Pieces of what used to be my heart,
Now shattered by your hands
The same hands that once held it like a their most prized possession.
Your words fell empty…
No longer filled with the passion that once stuck to me like glue.
Your emotions as distant as the Appalachian trail.
I pull you closer, you push me away
Establishing where you stand
The 'US' separated into You and I
I don't really understand…
How could you go from "I want us."
To "I'm not sure about how I feel."
In a matter of days?
How could the very same lips that said that, kiss me so deeply my soul fell in love again?
The same fingers you typed those words with set my skin on fire.
I don't understand what you mean by "unsure"
How can you be unsure in something YOU chose to pursue?
How dare you give a dream painted on clouds,
Then exchange it, leaving me scarred, covered in dirt?
You could've left me alone.
You could've let me be who I was and grow on my own
You should have left me alone.

Fondest Memories (in love)

When I felt safeness in other people.
When I felt secure in baring all my scars and flaws without feeling judged.
All our points of non-sexual intimacy.
The small things.
Moments where I was able to look around and think "these are the people I want in my life forever."
Laughs over drunken card games, loud off-key karaoke, exchanges of lipsticks & eyelash glue. Passing around of wine bottles as we hear Deena and Effie argue in the background.
Jumping on beds in onesies and listening to them talk about their thoughts.
Wine drunk affirmations and lists of things we are thankful for.
Giant bonnets and Toni Braxton songs.
Singing songs from 'Sister Act 2' as little footprints dance along in your womb.
Daily nap dates from states away and shared sides of the bed when you return home.
Watching them walk across the stage to graduate. The person I'd known since they were 15 was a little lady now.
Modeling her way through college that Rosebud is a beautiful flower.
Looking up and realizing that the woman who birthed me was not only my role model but one of my best friends
Shared photo albums and a few laughs.

Pushing me to be the best I could be.
The scent of the cologne left on your red jacket
Motivating me.
Being able to cry in front of them without hearing "you cry about everything."
Friends who motivate you to accomplish your dreams.
My favorite memory is an unspoken understanding of emotions and them reminding you that you'll be okay no matter what.
That you're loved no matter what

19/29/1

I have a theory. Not really a theory, but still. We always hear about karma and how it comes back around or how it can skip you and come to your kids. But what about if your kids get an aspect of your karma by watching you. My parents had me as teenagers, so expecting them to be mature or full grown about their marriage and certain things is a bit implausible. They dated, had me, got married, my dad went into the marines; a typical-seeming story.

But when my parents split, I was also still young. So, I never fully understood why, and I had a lot of questions. Why didn't they work out? Why didn't they try harder? Why wasn't my dad coming home anymore? I remember one day, I was about 6 or 7, and I was at my grandmother's house. My dad had this box with pictures in it. My mom, my godmother, different people. All smiling and happy, and there was this one picture of this woman in there. She was lying on her stomach with a t-shirt on that was too small and her butt was partially out. And she was flirtatiously looking at whoever was taking the picture. I remember thinking "Who is this?" But growing up in a black household, you're told to "Stay in a child's place." You don't question adults. You don't repeat what you see or hear etc. So, I kept flipping through the pictures and I found more pictures of her. I never told my dad about that.

When I got older, my dad and I fell out and then became close again. We would hang out and drink and smoke at times. We even talked about the times he cheated on my mother in a few moments. I don't think he meant to just reveal it, he was more so reminiscing about how childish he used to be. And it hit me. I don't want a partner like my father. I love him, but I also know that I deserve more than he gave my mother. In the same breath, I realized I was turning into my mother. I spend so much time trying to not be in the position that my mom was in. I feel like if I love harder or be the best person I can be, that'll keep them around. If I cling and love as hard as I possibly can, they'll stay. OR I shut down. I push people so far away because if they can't love me and if I don't love them, I won't get hurt. I've been spending so much time trying to not find someone like him that I never thought about trying not to become the person who went through the pain. I spent times hearing my mom cry or wondering who she was so angry towards him. And it took me having this moment to realize that maybe she wasn't angry, she was hurt.

I've been reflecting lately on my last few situationships and relationships, and that's what I did. I either pushed or pulled. And at the time I didn't realize it, but I also understand now. My mother is 38 years old and one of the most independent women I've ever known. As long as I can remember she's been independent. She's always made things happen. She's now at this point where she's learning not to be so independent and it's a process for her because it's scary. As a young woman watching her grow up, that's what I learned; to do things on my own and make them happen for myself. The only person I genuinely go to for help is her. So, I have some habits that I must unlearn and reteach myself, in a healthy manner. I'm working on finding comfort in solitude. I'm working on learning non-attachment but simultaneously not become so independent that I forget it's okay to love and be loved and that I don't have to do everything on my own. I'm also trying to balance being present and living for now, with planning for the future. I'm just trying to find what it is that I genuinely need.

Ellipsism

What is really the point?
We live this very full life,
Accompanied by hardships and accomplishments.
Some lives with more pain than others,
Some people's accolades bigger than others,
But what's really the point?
What happens when all is said and done?
When we close our eyes for eternal rest,
When life goes on with us and we become a part of history…
A part that won't even get to see how it impacted others.
Then what?
We all feel like our lives are so big and broad, but really, they're just a form of occhiolism.
Let's take a moment to bask in the moment.
Is time really of the essence?
Or is time the biggest lie to exist?
You can't measure moments in minutes or seconds.
You can't rush things or have this sense of urgency.
Take it all in.
Enjoy it

Conversations with self: Affirmations & Manifestations

I decided to do this daily ritual:
When I wake up in the morning, I look in the mirror and say 5 to 10 things I love about myself and before I go to bed at night, I list 5 to 10 things I'm grateful for.
The first time I did this it threw me off. My best friend Taylor and I were on facetime and she said, "Right now, list 10 things you're thankful for." And I started, but I think I got stuck on number 8. A few days later a twitter mutual of mine named Jessie told me to list 10 things I loved about myself. Now it sounds so easy, but the first time I did it, I realized I didn't have 10 things I loved about myself. So, I said, "let me just do 5…" I couldn't even list 5. It was in that moment I realized "this is a problem." So, I had these sticky notes that I'd write things on like "I am beautiful, I love myself." I later learned what affirmations were. I also learned not only how to properly affirm myself, but also the people that I love. You never know what internal struggles people have but sometimes that boost is what they need. You never know how much small words can help someone or brighten their mood. A simple "You are loved. You're doing great. I'm proud of you." can go so far in someone's life. It may not seem like much, but it is. Someone could be about to hit rock

bottom, and those few words can be helpful. I'm not putting a responsibility on anyone to do this daily; hell, I don't even do it daily. I just think it's important we know the role we play. Not only that, but also knowing the power of the tongue. For all my religious people, there's a scripture in your book. I'm unsure of your religion, but I was raised in a Christian household. So, in the bible it's Proverbs 18:21 "The tongue has the power of life and death, and those who love it will eat its fruit." There is life and death in what you speak. How many times have you said something so many times jokingly, then it came to fruition? Manifestations are real. Speak it, believe it, see it, do it.

18/22/9

I'm not her.
I am not the woman that broke you
I am not the woman that scarred you and left you with fragments.
I'm not the one who hurt you.
Stop pushing me away.
Stop penalizing me for a crime I didn't commit,
While the culprit runs free and you're left harboring the pain.
Her past mistakes and decisions are not mine,
So, by no means get the two confused.
I know the woman I am.
I know what I bring to the table, hell I built it.
I know what it is to love someone out of the hell they've been in,
To be their emotional punching bag
To be a distraction but not helping them heal.
I've been on both sides.
Understand that's not the role I intend to play,
Nor is it the part I auditioned for.
When I said I was here for whatever I meant it.
But I can't fully be present if you only partially open the door

Plans

I have plans for you.
To nourish you and help you grow.
To motivate you to be the best version of you possible.
Plans to be your friend amongst it all
To nurture you and protect you like your mother.
To love you as the Lord allows.
Apply salve to your scars and help them heal
To support you on your journey because I'm merely an accomplice.
To give laughter and love.
Please understand I'm speaking intentionally when I say
I have plans for you…

Equanimity

She was seemingly unbothered
Levelheaded, composed
She didn't get riled up at what "they" said
Never gave a second glance to the negativity
See they love to say Queens don't move off their thrown for peasantry
But she's not on a throne.
More, her root chakra won't be thrown off.
Her third eye won't be closed by meaningless mess and
Her crown chakra won't be shifted.
She is balanced.
Confident in the woman that she is.
Unmoved by chaos, instead she takes charge
She's strong
Poised throughout the most anarchic moments.
She takes charge
A leader
Forget being a queen, she birthed and built the nation.
So how dare she allow it to be what tore her down.
They spat upon scripture and tried to desecrate her genesis.
But she stood firm. Composed. Unbothered. Unmoved.
And soon they bowed at her feet.

Daydreams in love

I want to go to Paris.
Let me rephrase that.
Because those words lack the emotional experience I want.
See, I want to visit Paris with whoever it is I'll spend the rest of my life with.
As cheesy as it is, I want to visit the lock bridge.
I want to write our names on a lock, put it on there & throw away the key.
I want to write love letters & lock them away so that when times get hard,
I can use them as a reminder to why I'm with them and why I'll continue to fight for them through whatever.
I want to take pictures that tell the story of our love.
OUR story.
Of how you're not only my other half, you're my Best friend.
I want to have a special song & celebrate the anniversaries that aren't really anniversaries.
I want to walk down the aisle to Jesse Powell singing 'You'
Into the arms of someone who'll never let me know what it's like to not be held again.
And on our 25th anniversary, I want to go back to Paris to see our lock.
I want to think about everything we've gone through and be happy.
Because we made it through.

I want to cherish every situation because it was all worth it.
Each year shed each argument, each night we fought to keep loving.
I want to grow old and write our story down.
And I don't want to publish it.
But instead, give it to our children so they can know what love is.
Love isn't the pictures or the posts. Love is a fight.
Love is a battle and sometimes our hearts die in the process.
But as long as your partner is by your side, you'll never have to fight that battle alone.

Papa

I dreamt of you last night
Smelled your cologne and the faint stench of tobacco from your cigarettes
I was a small child running into your arms
Feeling the thick wool of your jacket
Watching old VHS tapes together
You're allowing me to do your hair.
And by doing your hair I mean slathering a jar of grease and some barrettes in it
Asking you "Grandpa, are you pretty?"
You always replied with a smile that reached your eyes.
There was so much you were supposed to see.
So much we were supposed to enjoy.
So much I wanted to do with you.
Now I have to do it for you.
And I'm going to do it all for you

Weary Anxiety

I'm tired mama
Why can't these thoughts just let me be?
I'm getting weak mama.
Day in and day out, I give and give and mama
I am empty.
I'm sorry mama.
Sorry I couldn't be someone who you were proud of.
Sorry that I had more fuck ups and slip-ups.
Sorry about the million times you had to lift me up.
I'm weary mama.
These demons are taking ahold of me mama
And tonight, I let them win

Doubts

I don't have to think when I'm with you
It amazes me how whenever I try to put my walls up you break them down
I'm just praying you actually stick around.
I'm so used to need a title or some form of security,
So, this whole 'going with the flow' thing is new to me
But it feels so right
Just don't leave with my heart in your pocket like some thief in the night.
I mean, I know love isn't all smiles and laughter
It's not the fairytale we imagine and believe as kids will happen
I know it's a fight and sometimes love is war
But my heart has been cupid standing in a war zone for so long I'm not really sure I can take anymore
I want the courage to love you freely
To not be possessive or needy, or afraid you won't need me
You'll do what everyone else does and leave me
I can't stop the rush of emotions
But I know that I love how the motion of our passion seems everlasting
So, for the time being, I'll push my doubts aside to create magic

Avalanche

Feelings fall
Emotions engulf you like Sunday dinner
The leave you feeling as torn as Saturday night drinking ...
Thoughts swallow you whole,
Anxiety spits you into the darkness where you lie with your demon's barren ...
1... 2... 3... you count the days
Quietly reminding yourself to breathe in, breathe out.
Automated... feed yourself so you don't starve
Breathe so you don't die
Smile so no one sees what's wrong
And pray that if they do see it, they don't ask.
Shed tears in the privacy of your own room
An old roommate once told me to cry in the shower because you can't distinguish the tears from the water.
Fight until all the fight in you is gone.
And when it's gone,
You go too...

Cravings

I crave intimacy. Not sex, but intimacy. Just physical contact and closeness. Mainly in the middle of the night, and it's the most annoying thing ever. I'll be fine during the day and at night I was to feel all these things like love and appreciation. I want to feel special and felt. I want forehead kisses and to be held. It's worse when you get the slightest taste of those things and then they get taken from you. I come home nightly to an empty bed, not an empty home. I love my family, but it isn't the same. I spend days at work, I pour myself into my art, I give love to myself and frankly' it's like playing kickball by yourself, tiring. In a perfect world right now, I'd be perfecting my craft. Studying what I love in some apartment or loft with white walls, not the dingy white but the really crisp white. Grey and black furniture decorating the living room. My art hanging on the walls throughout. A rose gold and cool grey themed bedroom with a faux fur rug on the floor in front of the bed. A cool grey comforter and sheet set with rose gold decorative pillows. Shared with someone I love and who loves me and a small puppy. I also want a room where I could do yoga, meditate, and paint. A serene room with a bookshelf, green plants, and a cute hanging chair so I can sit and read. See I have this mapped out in my head already. The chair will go right next to the window so I can look outside from it. IT's crazy how we always get told: "don't be in a rush to grow up." But I look forward to the days of being "washed". The days of spending time with the person who genuinely loves me and vice versa. Yet, sometimes I feel like that'll never happen. Like, maybe this love that I desire doesn't exist. Maybe I've watched 'The Notebook' and 'Love Jones' one too many times and I've created this entire perception of love that may not actually exist…

Blazes

I never understood why people get so close to you then pull away.
Taking a piece of you that you'll never get back
And after you repair yourself someone else seemingly does it again.
But the truth is,
Some people can't handle the heat from your fire.
No matter how much they love to watch the flames dance.

Vows

When I was a little girl, I used to imagine what I'd say to the person I'd spend forever with. My vows. My promises. Vows were something always poetic to me, so I needed to find the right words. I must've spent hours thinking and I came up with this.

"I've spent years thinking about this moment. Preparing for it. So, I'd know just what to say to make this moment "perfect". I knew I'd say something like "you're the second piece of the holy trinity of women in my life, next to my mother and our future daughter." Then I'd tell you how each moment we spend together eulogizes a moment forever engraved in my heart. How I know love is not all kind words, affection, and cuddles, and how I know bad times will come. But in those moments, I still keep my promise to be honest. I'm far from perfect but I'll still be the best I can for and to you. To love you even when I don't particularly like you. To communicate without belittling you. To fight over covers and bed space. To be not only your wife, but also your protector, best friend, and confidant. To not raise my voice or shut you out. To allow you to love me in moments when I can't even love myself. What I don't promise is perfection. I can't promise an easy life. But what I do promise is someone who won't give up on you, who won't walk away when things get hard and who will build with you because I am invested in us."

That sounds so perfect. But when that time comes so will the words. So will the emotions and everything I need. Those vows are nice, but when that moment comes my vows will be more… because my partner will deserve more.

Men

You scare me
Maybe it's because I know what you're capable of.
Always having the upper hand because of your gender,
You can get away with almost anything.
Not a care in the world so you don't hide your lewd remarks or wandering eyes as you mentally undress me.
No regards for permission so you reach out to a body that doesn't belong to you.
Rejection is followed by slurs and insults
"Bitch you ain't that cute anyway."
Or persistence because you believe women are playing hard to get.
You have no regard for women other than your mother or child, so you see them as disposable objects.
Toys to do with what you want.
Not even safe in their own workspace
Or checking a got damn mailbox
And this isn't about all of you.
But damn near all of you scare me.
I don't like being alone with men. It makes me panic.
My stomach clenches, my heart races and I feel like I don't inhabit my body anymore.
"Y'all over exaggerate, just say no"
Then what? When no isn't accepted, what do I do?

Cierra Antoinette   Letters I'll Never Send

Because clearly some of you missed that class on consent.
Predatorial behaviors coupled with misogyny and toxic masculinity.
I fear for my brothers becoming you…

Providence

I lie in the still of the night.
Taking a moment to reflect on the last 10 to 12 months
I lost things materialistically,
I had a financial plight.
I lost a few long-term friends,
In the same space finding out what they really thought of me.
It's amazing how someone can be in your corner, simultaneously looking at you as "beneath them."
Give some people space to help you and they never let you forget it.
Help those same people and they suddenly have amnesia.
I didn't understand what was happening at the time.
I didn't understand that things were aligning and opening up for me.
I didn't get that maybe I needed to lose things to get to where I'm going.
To gain a support system that is unquestionable.
To gain friends who push me to be a better me and accomplish my dreams daily.
Not only that, I found love when I wasn't looking.
A love that is patient and kind.
One that is understanding of me and my needs.

Not only a companion but one of my best friends.
This love may not be my forever, because I can't see the future.
But this love showed me that the love I've been praying for exists.
I've grown in so many ways
I've seen new perspectives.
Years ago, I never imagined I'd be this person
Genuinely happy
I still have growing to do.
But for once I can actually see how all things worked in my favor.

Antisocial Socialist

You know that one person who is friendly,
But hates being around people?
That's me.
My social battery drops quicker than
And I absolutely suck at not showing it.
I have a better chance at sneaking to get a
piece of cake out of that plastic container at 2 am,
Than I do of people not seeing my mood has changed.
I love people, but I love my alone time more.
And there are very few people I like to share my alone time with.
There are very few people I like to know me genuinely.
In public, I become this more polished version of myself.
"Sit up straight, mindful of how loud you laugh,
Don't open your mouth too wide, they'll see your gap.
Stay where you belong."
I do these things without thinking,
Being groomed between family and former lovers to be that 'perfect' version of myself.
That's 45% of what drains me alone.
The next 25% of that comes from interacting with people.
Forcing a conversation when in all honesty I want to be in my bed,

Cierra Antoinette   Letters I'll Never Send

In a giant t-shirt, eating pizza and watching a Law & Order: SVU marathon.
Oddly enough, when I'm doing that exact thing, I crave company.
And by that, I just mean someone to lay beside me.
DON'T SPEAK. DON'T MAKE CONVERSATION.
Simply enjoy the time with me…

I'm literally a walking contradiction

Final Wishes

If I close my eyes today or tomorrow, I want to be remembered for helping someone's life for the better. At least one person.
I want a small intimate homegoing service, surrounded by people I actually loved and who loved me. I don't want a sad service, sing one or two gospel songs in my favor, then tell your favorite memory of or with me. Cremate me and spread my ashes either in Paris or Egypt in the Nile River. And lastly, live. Live for me. Take whatever we went through and live your best life. That's all I ask.

Forgiveness vs. Healing

A sentence we often misuse is "I forgive you."
Mistaking it as synonymous for "I've healed."
In order to successfully move on you have to do both.
You can't truly heal without forgiving.
That's like trying to chop a tree with a plastic knife.
Forgiveness is just that, accepting the apology of /
Or the wrongdoing against you.
Healing is taking those steps to get back where you were.
Trusting. Rebuilding piece by piece
Not letting the past bound you any longer.
It's taking a step onto that limb.
You can't heal without forgiving,
But if you forgive and never heal,
That moment holds you hostage.

October 30

I caught myself getting mad because I wasn't coming home to you
Which is odd because I've never even been in your arms
And honey I'm patient,
As patient as the moon when it sets to let the sunshine
Just as the moon, I'll step back to let you shine
Because you deserve it.
You deserve to shine as people stare in awe.
But you instead choose to eclipse yourself behind what they want you to be.
You hide behind this mask but bare yourself to me
The scars you find hideous, are beautiful.
You are beautiful.

Conversations with self: Inspiration

Years ago, I learned what it felt like to be an inspiration…
To be a muse for someone.
As an artist, I always used others for inspiration or as a muse.
I'll never forget that poem
Or how I felt reading it, knowing it was for me…
That's a feeling I want forever…
To feel like I'm loved so much, I inspire you.
To be a piece of artwork in your eyes no matter how badly I think my canvas is ruined.

Note to self

Boundaries are important. Not only for others to set, but for you to set for yourself as well. You know better than anyone what triggers certain reactions or feelings. Look out for you and your best interest. Love yourself more.

You are just as important

3:34 am

People like you don't date women like me
You don't pick out the sapiosexuals who feign intellect
You don't go for the women who are too shy to speak up
You pick the women whose presence us known
Not a mere backdrop in the room
The ones who break heads and turn necks
People like you don't date women like me…
You may notice us,
But you continue moving…
We're relatively small in that light
And that's okay
Because people like you don't date women like me.
Women who create art out of you.
Who don't mind watching from the bleachers.
Who doesn't want to be on your arm every minute of the day.
We're complete opposites, but it makes sense
You bring me out of my shell,
I bring you off of that high.
Not too bad for someone who doesn't date women like me.

Conversations with self: Feelings

My favorite movie is 'The Notebook.' I think a lot of people get caught up in the ending and the sadness, but it's so much more than that. Their love was so much more than that. They spent a summer together. People from two completely different sides of the social spectrum. They built a love that wasn't necessarily perfect, but it worked for them. They fought all the time, but fighting didn't take away from how beautiful their love was. When her parents separated them, he still tried. 'A letter a day for a year', that's what he did. And even then, he wrote a final farewell. They both went on and lived their lives until fate bought them back together. 7 years later, but it still bought them together again. I'm a hopeless romantic if you can't tell. Stories like this give me hope. They make me feel like, even though things go wrong, love isn't in vain. What's meant to be will always be. They give me hope in the 'right person, wrong time.' quote. They also give me hope that maybe the love I believe in exists. I can't really afford to think it doesn't. I can't make myself believe that love is painful or staying around when someone treats you wrong. I can't make myself believe that love is settling for anything less than someone who gives you the butterflies 20 years later. My dad's parents have been married for over 30 years. Do you know how rare that is? Even more rare that my grandfather can still make my grandma laugh like a sixteen-year-old girl and she's almost 70. I look at them with admiration because I know it wasn't the easiest thing, but they did it. They still love one another genuinely. They still make each other smile. They're each other's best friend. To know that there are people in the world who never will get to experience that or who settle for less… I can't be one of them.

I think that's also what scares me. I never want to feel like I'm settling, but I also never know if someone is 'the one'. I've thought about it before and been wrong. I don't want to be wrong anymore. So, I always leave a little bit of space, some people call them back up plans. It's never intentional. The grass isn't greener on either side, it's green where you water it and put in the effort. But what if this lawn isn't mine? I've realized… I'm my own problem. I'm so scared of the 'what if's' that I don't enjoy the moment. "What if they don't love me back? What if they find better? What if they realize I'm not what they want?"

what if I stopped listening to what if's…

Devotee

I'm a firm believer that the person for you won't ever make you choose between them and your dreams. Your dreams may not align, but they'll always be a supporter on your journey. Whether it's from right beside you or on the sideline.

Solitude

I'm learning to be comfortable in solitude
But not so engulfed in it that I become overly independent.
I always crave affection and intimacy
Yet, I don't like receiving it from my sole self.
I don't enjoy pouring into myself
I like loving others
I enjoy it beyond what I can express
Volcanos erupt after so many years of rest
The world is constantly evolving
People are constantly evolving
So, if there's something that can be constant…
Something that can help us get by a little more each day
Whether it's platonic or intimately,
Why not want to share it with others?
Why just harbor it for yourself?

10:54 pm

Understand that she's fragile
The smallest thing will cause her to shut down...
She's apologetic for things that aren't even her fault.
Look in her eyes and you'll see every piece of her broken soul.
Touch her and you'll feel all the tenseness from her past pain
She may look strong
She may act strong
But she needs a nurturing touch
A gentle heart and someone patient enough to support her while she heals herself
She is damaged and she doesn't need anyone to fix her,
Just be there as she fixes herself

Besoins

I wish that there was a way that I can bottle your pain.
That there was someone that I can ask to take all of your troubles away and give them to me
I wish I had the love that can be poured into your soul and wash out the hurt
When you lie awake at night with the memories taunting you,
Can I be the force to silence them?
To ease them until you're soothed.
When you feel backed into a corner, can I be there to help you escape?
If love can truly heal all things, just tell me how much you need
I'll give you all of me if that ensures healing your brokenness
Because darling, sleeping has never been painful until the one that I love couldn't
Smiling was never accompanied by weight on my heart until a love of mine found it hard to do so
My happiness was never up for exchange until yours went missing.
And my soul never searched so hard for solutions until it was what you needed.

Sapiosexual

Words dance across the nape of my neck
Your voice lingers in my ear, the perfect aphrodisiac
Your tree bears fruit that feeds this hunger I have
It quenches my thirst to know more
Tantalizing and delicious.
Your words caress me
They reach around and slowly undress all of my inhibitions
Simultaneously parting my thoughts,
Entering each of them deliberately and intensely
Pushing me to be a better woman with each thrust
Release sustenance and authenticity in me and watch what I birth
I am begging you for more
Aroused by the intellect you possess
Your lips speak words to me that wrap around my throat
Then lean against my lips gently
as you breathe life into each hope and dream that I have
Every endeavor and venture I step into,
You've been my number one fan
Forever letting me know it's possible
You send me poetic lines that send chills down my spine
As I drip in ecstasy

Cierra Antoinette   Letters I'll Never Send

Your mind gives me the greatest orgasm I've ever known
Speak as my river flows for you…

Just for you.

Dear Cierra

Dear Cierra,
I apologize to you. I apologize for every time I never believed in you. For every time I doubted you and wasn't there for you. I apologize for each time I didn't stand up for you. It wasn't your fault. You aren't to blame for what others did/didn't do to you. You weren't responsible for being the glue that held your family together, therefore it isn't your fault that the family broke. Your father loved you. He always has and always will, I apologize for ever making you doubt that. You're always been worth so much more than you give yourself. I apologize for ever putting it into your head that you deserved anything less. I apologize for listening to anyone who said you deserved anything less. I apologize for surrounding you with people who looked down on you while you admired them. Those people were not friends. I apologize for not giving you the credit you deserve and trying to make you what I wanted you to be and not the woman you were meant to be. I put so much emphasis on you being someone who everyone else loves that I forgot to be the one who loves you. Genuinely loves you. I apologize for making you so fearful of the future that you don't focus on the present. You are human and being afraid of failure is okay. Time is of the essence, but your hourglass should never be compared to anyone else's. I

apologize for viewing your worth through other people's eyes because that only lowered your self-worth and pushed you further away from who you really are. I apologize for not pushing you to know that everything you endure is for the better. Most of all, I apologize for being your worst enemy. I vow to be your biggest fan, number one lover and genuinely happy with who you're becoming.

Love,
Yourself

Buyer's Remorse

I wasn't looking for you.
I didn't even expect to pick you up off the shelf, but somehow you chose me.
The most beautiful picture I'd ever seen
Picasso had nothing on the God that created you.
You fit so well in the future I saw
But I guess that's what I get for planning ahead.
You came with beautiful but empty promises
The structure that they were built on withered away like flowers in the fall;
Slow, but once they were gone you stood bare.
I wanted you to be the perfect décor for the home in my heart
But maybe I have homesickness for a home that never really existed
I was building a home and you were just renting…
I've always had an affliction for injudicious purchases,
Usually grabbing what catches my eyes.
Not so much paying attention to the price tag.
I didn't plan on returning you,
I just knew you'd be mine forever
But this time I thank God that I kept the receipt…

Groundkeeper

I don't want to be just your friend.
Call me a bit unreasonable, but I never intended on that.
I planted seeds in you for us to grow.
Watered my grass so it was green, so maybe I don't understand why I'm lying in barren soil.
Dry as the desert after I put in so much work.
You let me plant these seeds.
Promised me to be sunlight and fertilizer.
That we would grow this garden together,
Now it's nowhere in sight.

I stand in my own garden.
It's not perfect, not even close.
It still needs tending to.
The weeds need to be pulled and it needs to be trimmed.
I could always clean it up,
But the work I put into "our" garden,
I should've put it into my own.
Relying on someone else to build your vision is unfair.
Forcing someone else to pour into you what you give to them is unfair.
And that's okay.
These days, I vow to water myself.
To put more time into my own flowers growing.
I'm in control of my garden.
My green thumb may not have been right for that, but I'll practice for myself.

Cierra Antoinette   Letters I'll Never Send

I hold no animosity towards you.
Someday we may cross paths again.
And when that day comes,
I'll admire your garden from my side and
laugh at memories of ours.
I'll be thankful for those moments.
Because they pushed me to get back to me

Note from an Artist to an Artist

Remember this the next time you feel something strongly. Whether that emotion is good or bad. Your art can either suffer at the expense of your emotions, or you can create something more passionate than anything you've ever done. The choice is yours.

Je vous libère

I released you to the earth.
I sat down and wrote you.
Wrote of the symphonies your eyelashes played
Drew out the future I saw whenever I looked in your eyes.
Heard the beautiful song the voice of yours sang time and time again when you said, "I love you."
I smelled the scent of your cologne and envisioned the place I once knew as home.
I wrote you.
I made myself feel everything all over again.
Took myself down the path of reliving the good.
Touched all the leftover love marks.
Felt your lips against mine for the last time.
Chanted your name again and laughed at the secrets we shared.
I felt you.
I got down on my knees and prayed for healing.
Let go of the little hope I had left.
Packed your things, shipped them off
Said my final farewells.
All that was left for me to do was release you
I sat down with a pen and paper.
Ink always brings me to say the things I don't know how.
It's always been one of my best confidants.

Cierra Antoinette   Letters I'll Never Send

Placed letters on the page as they filled them, letting the emotions flow.
1, 2, 3, 4.
Held the pages to the flames and watched them transform into ash.
I released you to the earth.
I let go of all love and hurt.
Sought guidance and healing.
Cleansed my spirit and body,
Wore white for 3 days.
Charged my stones, used my oils, burnt my sage.
Focused on myself.
And I released you…
Unconfined.
Unrestrained.
No longer attached.

I release you…

Repressed Proclivities

Last night I dreamt of you.
You seemed worn.
A bit tired of the facade you put up.
You ached for me...
You were lonely yet surrounded by so much
Smiling over the emptiness...
Last night I dreamt you missed me...
As a creative, I've got a habit of picturing
things that don't exist.
Usually, I'm able to bring them to life.
But it was only a dream,
Right?

Petal Ballet

Delicate petals dance across the wind
As the breeze caresses them with a gentleness
never before seen
The sun as a spotlight, while you perform your
solo.
It's been a long winter.
Not one of extreme cold, yet you were the
only one to withstand it.
A soldier to be admired
The night and dance both the perfect
background.
The moon casting a dim light against you.
You remain beautiful in all aspects
When you're in full bloom and
When you wither away for a seasons rest
This is the life.
This is the beauty of what life has given.
You are the rose.
You're each petal and the world in your
background.
Don't ever be too afraid to dance…

3/9/2019

She asked "What inspires you? What's your muse?"
Other people, pain, pleasure.
"Why not yourself?"
I paused…
To me, poetry is about finding a way for self-expression.
It's a reflection of the beauty in all situations
I don't find attributes about myself particularly beautiful
I believe internally I resonate beauty…
But I'd rather find beauty in other things.
"What do you fear?"
Love.
It's the most beautiful thing to come across.
Yet it possesses the possibility of being one of the most painful things too.
It can be that flying carpet in Aladdin and the minute it slips from under you, you fall to something that could possibly break all that you are.

Bed of Deceit

I stand in the corner taking in an aesthetic I once loved.
Shocked at the thigs clarity could bring to light when you're no longer blinded.
My eyes land on our bed and the way it was built.
Presented as a gift for me, I was so excited I never even bothered to pay attention.
The wooden frame put together in a rush, with jagged nails and uneven wood.
Held together by the unsteady glue of promises said during infatuation.
I guess this is where the splinters came from every morning I got up.
I never saw them coming.
Moving onwards to the box spring underneath the mattress.
It was built of bandages and buts, yet still had springs sticking out of it.
Coiled things like trust issues, I tried to ignore but after a while, you just can't.
The mattress sat there. The mattress cover over it resonates love and compassion, promising a future and a gentle, safe place to lie every night.
I peel it back, staring at the mattress built on indecisiveness, unsureness.
Riddled on one side with "I don't know if I want you, but I know I don't want anyone else to have you."

Cierra Antoinette — Letters I'll Never Send

The other sprinkled with alternating spots of
"I want this" and "Nah I'm good on you."
I stare at the wasted wine on the floor.
Sweet nothings drain from the glass sitting on the table.
Each droplet a reminder of the drunken love you spew at 1 am
Just to take back when you wake up.
I've never wished for a hangover until now…
I stare in the mirror, tired of a war with myself.
I could clean up the wine but that's the part of this picture I love most
At any moment I could stand to my feet and walk away,
But each time I get to the door I think "maybe I can beautify this place."
Rub sandpaper along the bed frame, put more wine into the glass.
I believe we're deeper than all of this, yet I have a fear of false hope.
I know I want you.
Without reason or stipulation.
I know I can't make it be reciprocated.
So, I leave you to rebuild your own bed.
And I'll go lie in my own.

Self-Medicating

I mingle through a crowd,
wishing I could appreciate the atmosphere a
bit more,
But the truth is everything in here reminds me
of you.
I see your face on every person's body
Smell the scent of bourbon in the air and hold
back tears.
Hands feel like hands in the dark.
Bodies pressed upon bodies,
But none of these voices belong to you.
It's unhealthy to surround yourself with things
you're trying to heal from.
A recovering alcoholic wouldn't sit in a bar
An addict who's withdrawn wouldn't sit in the
lab
But how can I escape when you are
everywhere?
It's like trying to breathe and you are the very
thing that is drowning me
I JUST WANNA BE LEFT ALONE
Stop writing me these letters
Forget my address, let me breathe
Let me go back to before any of this ever
existed
I'm tired of the side effects.
Yet I can't seem to turn my location off
Or delete this damn joint album.
The pictures from my vacation.
The message thread,
I still haven't erased your contact…

The problem is,
My drug of choice was you
Your love was the booster and
I was medicating way more than I needed
And this… this is the hardest withdrawal ever

Truth

Fingers often get pointed when both people are to blame.
The truth is, I didn't kick you out of our bedroom…
no matter how messy it was, no matter if our bed wasn't made.
You chose to get up and walk away.
And I got tired of begging you to stay,
so, I didn't ask you to come back anymore…
I didn't even bother trying to clean it up to your liking.
I turned off the lights, closed the door, and place my key beside yours.

Vending Machine

I make my way to you
Coins in hand, a nagging a snack
Not so much because I'm hungry, but because I'm bored.
And snacking seems like a good idea
I stare at the options.
Searching for which one of them will satisfy me temporarily,
Being that none of them hold any actual substance
Eyes browse over bars of candy which create cavities
So sweet yet so damaging
Kind of like your love.
Chips and Knick Knacks.
Yes? No.
They have more air in the bag than actual chips.
I wish I had thought about loving you this hard.
I wish I had realized that no matter how good you tasted,
I'd always crave more.
That I'd paid attention to what I was feeding myself,
Because I would've saved myself a lot.
I mean, we usually can't confuse a snack for a meal.
Yet I did.
Looking for quick nutrients like love and affection

Cierra Antoinette   Letters I'll Never Send

Remember what you put into your body
matters
Back away from the vending machine and sit
at the dinner table
Indulge in healthy sugars like fruit
And a love that's just as sweet and healthy.
As filling as dinner on Thanksgiving.
Understand that you're worth more than a
snack
And walk away from the vending machine

Ode to The Burg

Bowl. Strike. March.
History surrounds us.
Festivals atop massacres to celebrate
bloodshed and roses blooming.
Color walls hidden by shops,
803 branded with pride on different structures
Our version of Os Gemeos mural
Unions in the most unforeseen places,
Like breakfast at the local gas station.
The occasional mug across the fairgrounds
But still being able to chill with your people.
My little town is one that I love
To the eye, we may just be some old historical place
No movie theatre, a tiny mall, and not many restaurants
From the streets of Goff Avenue to Hillcrest.
Past Walmart to 301.
Biddy's banquet, The Rose festival, Jammers, Edisto Gardens
The history behind our little bowling alley
Both Claflin and South Carolina State University.
This is an ode to Orangeburg.
Talent lines these streets
Friends starting families
Our parents all friends as we're being raised together
The cycle continuing because
We're one.

Cierra Antoinette   Letters I'll Never Send

We come together in our greatest and worse times.
Because despite it all, we're a family.
We're all burg babies

Simply Being

I'm not a fan of being,
Or of simply existing.
I don't like questions with answers that are personal.
Or ones that I don't know the answer to.
Don't ask me about school…
Don't make commentary on how I don't go to church every Sunday.
I don't like myself.
I am the most brutal bully I could ever have.
I need to be in someone's gym.
Physically I'm not the most attractive.
Maybe a 4 on a scale of 1-10.
I just have a big butt, I'm talented and I'm smart,
So that bumps me up to a smooth 7.
My confidence is outweighed by my self-doubt and insecurities.
I look for confirmation in my friends, family, and lovers.
Hoping that they validate me without asking,
Because that means I'm doing a bit better today than usual.
Hoping to hear them say they're proud because
Maybe all my searching for self isn't in vain.
Maybe I'm doing at least one thing right to earn their approval
Constantly comparing myself to those around me because

Cierra Antoinette — Letters I'll Never Send

I'm surrounded by constant beauty and can never match the energy
Finding solace on the internet because just enough likes will soften these voices
I've become good at masking the way I look at me.
Avoidance tangos with me daily.
I'm not my number one fan, I'm not a fan at all.
Just a spectator in the middle waiting to see how it turns out.
I apply enough makeup to make myself seem at least decent.
Covering each negative comment to myself with foundation,
Concealing them then packing them with powder
Lining each lie and filling in the gaps where I believe I lack.
I've become so good at locking myself in a box and swallowing the key
Because the person I really am isn't good enough for anyone's eye
Let alone good enough to be loved unconditionally.
My dark humor carries the uncertainties when my box becomes too full.
Overflowing all the ugly parts of me that I worked so hard to hide.
I'm still learning to apologize to myself for all my wrongdoings.

Still learning to forgive myself so how dare I ask anyone else for an apology.
Still figuring out how to not feel so bad for waking up in the morning and
believing I look somewhat decent.
Educating myself on how to take a compliment without thinking it's genuinely a mockery.
Still failing these courses like I did my sophomore year of college.
Hoping one day I'll wake up and someone else will be looking back at me in that mirror.
Someone I can be proud of.
Someone who doesn't have to hide these things from the people who love her.
Someone who doesn't think the people who love her only do it because they have to.
I cry in the shower.
I don't need to hear "you cry too much"
And thank God those walls don't speak to me.
They can't tell me each flaw that riddles my body that I already know exists
so, I avoid looking at myself naked
My siblings look up to me and I wish I knew why they did
Because I'm not even sure why I exist.
I wish there were a form of makeup for the insides instead of diluting who I am.
I wish I could operate on my own heart because all that ugliness carries over into it
And it's never me being unhappy with anyone else,

Cierra Antoinette   Letters I'll Never Send

It's me being unhappy with myself but lord knows I can't even fix my lips to say it.
I can never let anyone know those parts of me.
I can never speak on the conversations I have with myself in the still of the night.
Each night in my bed.

Nostalgia II

I'm a very nostalgic being
I have a clear affliction for pain,
Because I love to relive my most painful moments.
Like a child picking at a scab or me with my acne
I stroll down memory lane from top to bottom,
Then again in reverse.
Skimming my fingers across years of things
Some I can feel more intense than others
Some I can barely feel but still remember vividly.
Those aren't scabs anymore, just scars
Bruises amongst discolored skin
Battle wounds from a soldier who stepped on the field,
My heart often the only weapon I preferred
Yes, it's been through some things,
But it's still the only weapon I need.
It's seen as many high's as it's seen low's
A little worn, but by all means still pure.
Still whole and still beating.
I've fought battles alongside friends, family, and lovers.
Turned around and fought battles against those same people
Understand I am not new to this,
I still make mistakes, but I am a veteran in this game of life
My heart, still my greatest weapon.
My art, this art,

The product of my PTSD
Proof that beauty comes from all things and
That love never really fails,
It only cultivates and molds you for greatness.
My nostalgia is a museum dedicated to my strength.
My nostalgia is a monument dedicated to my growth
It's not about the pain or happiness baby
It's about what it birthed

Impatient

Patience is a virtue the Lord knows I don't possess.
Give me an outline and itinerary and I expect to follow it to a T
I don't believe in being late so in my mind,
On time is late and early is on time.
Seconds and minutes tango with my anxiety
Both fighting to be the lead
Here comes my inept desire to just say "fuck it" and sleep,
Searching for a chance to cut in.
My breathing skills and grounding meditations forgotten slowly on the sideline
As I watch this ongoing battle.
Searching for a way to end it with the forgotten as the leads,
And the leads as the forgotten.
Grandma always told me time is a figment of our imagination,
That time itself doesn't really exist; clocks exist.
But the hourglasses stand side by side
The 24 hours in one and my need to do 525,600 things in those hours
A years' worth of tasks in a day because
I want to accomplish so much before my time runs out.
It's not that I'm impatient.
I've lost people who died before they even got the chance to live.

Cierra Antoinette   Letters I'll Never Send

The death of someone close to or my age
every year since I was 10.
Time isn't something I take for granted
because,
Unlike an hourglass when my time runs out…
I don't get to flip it and start over.

Road Tripping

There's nothing you can tell me I don't know about myself.
I am my own biggest critic.
Brutally honest with myself.
I hurt my own feelings so no one else has the chance.
Believe me when I say I've told myself it all
"You're a prude"
"You aren't that smart"
"You need to be in someone's gym"
"Your friends keep you around because they feel sorry for you and you make them look better."
This list can go on longer than you'd ever imagine.
I wasn't always this insecure.
Somewhere in my adolescence, it started.
"Your mom is so pretty; you must look like your dad"
Was something I heard so much that whenever I didn't hear it,
I said it to myself.
When it comes to my friends, I shrink in the background
If I'm unnoticed, nobody will say anything because they can't
And I like it that way.
Let me be.
I don't particularly care for anyone else's views or criticism
Don't tell if I don't ask.

I'm already aware.
Let me battle my demons in peace.

A journey

So, we've almost reached the end of this book and I am in a space where creatively I'm at a standstill. Writing this book has taken a lot of being honest and open, not only with myself but with the reader. I'm not a person big on vulnerability, especially not when it comes to strangers. So, putting myself out like this has been a journey into a new space. It's also allowed me to find out and acknowledge many more things about myself than I knew previously. I am a work in progress. I still have a lot of healing that I didn't realize I had to do, but I'm also so grateful that it was bought to the surface so I can deal with it. When I first started writing this, I had this idea that it would be a closing chapter to things that I'd gone through. Instead, it's become the first step to a journey of healing that I need. This space I'm in is one that I couldn't go through before, because I hadn't accomplished the growth that I needed for it. Right now, I have an amazing support system, filled with family members and friends who have been pushing me to be the best version of myself. I've also become a person who is comfortable with their own problems because acknowledgment is vital. So, while this book was me sharing one journey with you all, it also became a doorway to another for me. I am appreciative of each person and situation that was an inspiration for this piece. Whatever the terms we were on, whatever happened, I thank you for pushing the growth. So, as I venture on this new path of healing and learning, I also let this one go.

To the reader

Years ago, if someone had told me that I'd be the author of a poetry book, I would've never believed them. I would've never believed that one, I was capable of something this great or two, anyone would care about the things I had to say. If you had told me that every trial and tribulation that I faced would become an inspiration; if you had told me that I'd grow into someone I am learning to love, I would've never believed any of it. I didn't even think I'd make it to see 21. I always had this feeling that I'd die young. But in that same belief, I never wanted to venture out of my comfort zone. This is that. This book didn't take as long as I thought. My hardest nights were the nights I had writer's block from either feeling entirely too much and not being able to process it or feeling nothing at all. Nonetheless, it happened. This is my baby. This is to the young girl that wondering who she's supposed to be, to the one going through a heartbreak she feels like she'll never get over, to the boy trying to fit in but not quite getting it: It is alright to make mistakes. It is okay to be unsure. You are doing great my love. Cry those tears, feel what you feel, learn who you are, and the rest will come. I am proud of you. I see you. I am you. I wrote this for you.

I want to thank whoever is reading this for their support also. I'm a pretty ordinary young lady. You would catch me walking down the street and not glance twice in my direction. That's the beauty of it though. I'm just a small-town girl with dreams and aspirations to inspire others. I hope this did that for you. I hope that when you put this book down, there's at least one piece that inspires or moves you in some way. I can't say for sure whether I'll write another or not. The future holds a great deal that is unknown. What I can say though, is the pieces of me that you've learned to appreciate are within you. We all go through hardships, but the healing and growth are already planted in you. Water them and grow something beautiful.

- Cierra Antoinette

Made in the USA
Columbia, SC
23 October 2024